Months of the Year

December

by Robyn Brode

Reading consultant: Susan Nations, M.Ed.,
author/literacy coach/consultant

WEEKLY WR READER®
EARLY LEARNING LIBRARY

Please visit our web site at: www.earlyliteracy.cc
For a free color catalog describing Weekly Reader® Early Learning Library's list
of high-quality books, call 1-877-445-5824 (USA) or 1-800-387-3178 (Canada).
Weekly Reader® Early Learning Library's fax: (414) 336-0164.

Library of Congress Cataloging-in-Publication Data

Brode, Robyn.
 December / by Robyn Brode.
  p. cm. – (Months of the year)
  Summary: An introduction to some of the characteristics, events, and activities
 of the month of December.
  ISBN 0-8368-3587-5 (lib. bdg.)
  ISBN 0-8368-3623-5 (softcover)
  1. December–Juvenile literature. 2. Holidays–United States–Juvenile literature.
 3. Winter–United States–Juvenile literature. [1. December.] I. Title.
 GT4803.B764 2003
 394.261–dc21   2002034321

First published in 2003 by
Weekly Reader® Early Learning Library
330 West Olive Street, Suite 100
Milwaukee, WI 53212 USA

Copyright © 2003 by Weekly Reader® Early Learning Library

Editor: Robyn Brode
Art direction, design, and page production: Leonardo Montenegro with Orange Avenue
Models: Olivia Byers-Strans, Isabella Leary, Madeline Leary
Weekly Reader® Early Learning Library art direction: Tammy Gruenewald
Weekly Reader® Early Learning Library editor: Mark J. Sachner

Photo credits: Cover, title, pp. 7, 11, 13, 15, 19, 21 © Getty Images; p. 9 © Gregg Andersen;
p. 17 Leonardo Montenegro

Printed in the United States of America

1 2 3 4 5 6 7 8 9 07 06 05 04 03

Note to Educators and Parents

Reading is such an exciting adventure for young children! They are beginning to integrate their oral language skills with written language. To help this process along, books must be meaningful, colorful, engaging, and interesting; they should invite young readers to make inquiries about the world around them.

Months of the Year is a new series of books designed to help children learn more about each of the twelve months. In each book, young readers will learn about festivals, celebrations, weather, and other interesting facts about each month.

Each book is specially designed to support the young reader in the reading process. The familiar topics are appealing to young children and invite them to re-read — again and again. The full-color photographs and enhanced text further support the student during the reading process.

These books are designed to be read within an instructional guided reading group. This small group setting allows beginning readers to work with a fluent adult model as they make meaning from the text. After children develop fluency with the text and content, the book can be read independently. Children and adults alike will find these books supportive, engaging, and fun!

— Susan Nations, M.Ed., author, literacy coach,
and consultant in literacy development

December is the twelfth and last month of the year. December has 31 days.

December 12

1	2	3	4	5	6	7
8	9	10	11	12	13	14
15	16	17	18	19	20	21
22	23	24	25	26	27	28
29	30	31				

In December, fall ends and winter begins. Winter usually begins on December 21.

When winter begins, the days are the shortest. It is dark for a much longer time than it is light.

In some places, it can get cold and snowy in December. There are lots of ways to enjoy the snow!

Some places do not have snow in December. It might even be warm. In places where it is warm, it is also fun to play outside.

Is it warm in December where you live?

In December, many kids take a break from school and have a winter vacation.

During the month of December, many families and friends get together to celebrate Hanukkah, Christmas, or Kwanzaa. Sometimes they give each other gifts.

December 31 is New Year's Eve. It is the last day of December and also the last day of the year.

When December ends, it is time for January to begin. Then the twelve months of the year begin all over again.

What do you think the new year will bring?

Glossary

New Year's Eve — the last night of the year; at midnight a new year begins

winter — a season that begins on the day it stays dark the longest

winter vacation — a time when schools take a break, usually for about two weeks

Months of the Year

1	January	7	July
2	February	8	August
3	March	9	September
4	April	10	October
5	May	11	November
6	June	**12**	**December**

Seasons of the Year

Winter	Summer
Spring	Fall

About the Author

Robyn Brode wrote the *Going Places* children's book series and was the editor for *Get Out!*, which won the 2002 Disney Award for Hands-On Activities. She has been an editor, writer, and teacher in the book publishing field for many years. She earned a Bachelors in English Literature from the University of California at Berkeley.